FOR ELIZA

MEET SELF-CONTROL

SELF-CONTROL IS CALM

SELF-CONTROL IS FOCUSED

SELF-CONTROL IS CAREFUL

WHEN SELF-CONTROL CAN FEEL SHE IS STARTING TO GET UPSET

SHE PAUSES

BREATHES SLOWLY

AND REACTS
APPROPRIATELY

WHEN SOMEONE ELSE IS TALKING

SELF-CONTROL FOCUSES HER EYES AND
EARS TO LISTEN AND UNDERSTAND
BEFORE SHE SPEAKS HERSELF

WHEN SELF-CONTROL SPEAKS

SHE KNOWS HER WORDS ECHO THROUGH TIME

SO SHE CHOOSES THEM WISELY

SHE GETS RIGHT TO WORK

STAYS FOCUSED

AVOIDS DISTRACTIONS

AND COMPLETES IT WELL

SHE LEARNS THE RULES

AND ALWAYS MAKES SURE SHE FOLLOWS THEM

WHEN SELF-CONTROL IS ALONE WITH HER IMAGINATION

SHE REMAINS CALM HERSELF

AND HELPS TO CALM THOSE AROUND HER AS WELL

SELF-CONTROL KNOWS THAT EVERY DAY THERE ARE SO MANY CHOICES

AND HOW DECISIONS WE MAKE CA DRASTICALLY IMPACT OUR LIVES

THE MOMENTS WHEN THESE CHOICES NEED TO BE MADE ARE OFTEN UNEXPECTED AND STRESSFUL

BY KEEPING OUR EMOTIONS IN CHECK WITH SELF CONTROL

WE CAN MAKE BETTER DECISIONS WHEN IT MATTERS THE MOST

IF YOU CAN ACT LIKE SELF-CONTRO

YOU ARE ON THE WAY TO HAVING BLACK BELT CHARACTER TOO

NEXT TIME WE WILL MEET
SELF-CONTROL'S FRIENDS!

Made in the USA
Columbia, SC
15 January 2021